T0128955

Enchanteur of Hearts

Enchanteur of Hearts

Ryan Carneiro

ENCHANTEUR OF HEARTS

iUniverse books may be ordered through booksellers or by contacting:

iUniverse
1663 Liberty Drive
Bloomington, IN 47403
www.iuniverse.com
1-800-Authors (1-800-288-4677)

Because of the dynamic nature of the Internet, any web addresses or links contained in this book may have changed since publication and may no longer be valid. The views expressed in this work are solely those of the author and do not necessarily reflect the views of the publisher, and the publisher hereby disclaims any responsibility for them.

Any people depicted in stock imagery provided by Thinkstock are models, and such images are being used for illustrative purposes only. Certain stock imagery © Thinkstock.

ISBN: 978-1-4917-9680-1 (sc)
ISBN: 978-1-4917-9679-5 (e)

Library of Congress Control Number: 2016909767

Print information available on the last page.

iUniverse rev. date: 06/13/2016

Contents

Intentional Fallacy: Introduction

I decided to write love poems to express the wonderful feelings and emotions I have regarding matters of the heart as they relate to reality. Basically I seek to link the world of imagination and the world of reality. Without any contradictions, my aim is to keep my readers in suspense and to make them be attentive, relaxed, calm, aware, and transcendent.

My poems make use of positive dialogue, illusions, improvisation, mystery, confusion, wonder, and bafflement. They bring to the reader's mind the fondness and happiness that can be discovered by people who are heartbroken. They inspire people to never stop pursuing a second chance to conquer or to be loved. Although we all experience hardships on account of love, to me love is the best emotion that any one of us can ever receive. By exploring love, I have been able to discover my own insights, which reflect—in collage and montage—passion, lust, desire, inspiration, motivation, ideas, style, commitment, irony, appreciation, confidence, liberty, and true love. Despite the criticism my poems have received, I find that writing poetry frees me to express what is in my conscious mind about true love. I regard love from a reader's perspective as well. As is commonly known, all good deeds are met by obstacles from other people, such as contempt, envy, jealousy, betrayal, desperation, infidelity, adultery, and other, unmentioned illicit feelings and behaviors. In the face of these things, I turn fondly to poetry to rid myself of such hindrances and to encourage my yearning to find a true love that will last until eternity.

As a poet, I seek to instill in the mind of anyone who is in love the idea that one should always conduct oneself with a pure intention, having no excuses but focusing on sharing love via sensuality, courtesy, belief, choice, interaction, and so forth, in order to attain boldness and care, which in turn will unite tradition with modern practices. Whether you, reader, are single, married, divorced, widowed, or still searching for true love, I, as a love poet, want to be your pillar of hope. I can be this pillar of hope if you lean on me while you pursue love on a secure, optimistic, supportive, honest, selfless, committed, sacrificial, give-and-take basis when dealing with emotional anguish, heartbreak, and infatuation, thereby ending up with the moral ability to prophesize that your loved one—and mine—will have serenity.

Restless without You

For each of the days of my life that have passed, I have held in mind a myth about my daily life experiences. Every time I try to figure out the myth, I get a cold shiver down my spine.

Since the time you and I crossed paths, I've realized that I have made happy changes to my life. After you and I first met, I was astonished to find that my myth had vanished and I was once again free, which made me, from that day forward, feel restless without you.

Comparing my past and present, I am at a standstill, with nowhere to go and with no one to share my thoughts with. Surrounded by worries, I feel like I am nailed to a cross.

I am in pain when you are absent. I end up in a dilemma, constantly wishing for everything else to disappear, since you are all I'll ever need henceforth. I am restless when I am without you.

Worldwide, people tend to proclaim that they are blessed. In my defense, I, as a Christian and a strong believer in the Holy Spirit, seek only the blessing of having you beside me on earth. With the Lord as my witness, I announce that I will give my all to you until death do us part, implying that I love you more than anything else and verifying again how restless I am without you.

The Woman Who Makes Me Happy

All of a sudden, with no absolutely clue of how I felt, you appeared in my life and made me the happiest man alive. Nothing has ever stunned me as much as that did.

It has been great strolling in this nice climate, which is unbelievable when compared to the hearty and dusty climate I escaped from a few weeks ago. And it's all because of you.

One makes choices after giving plenty of consideration and thought. My choices relate more to the various meals, including the desserts and the different appetizers and beverages, we shared together. You are the woman who makes me happy.

Bedazzler of My Soul

Today, being a long, hectic, stressful, hurtful, and resentment-inspiring day given the awful acts I saw committed, gave me a wake-up call and elucidated how empty and wounded I am without you in my life.

Nobody has ever been able to know the real me, because I am simple, evasive, and cautious in everything I do or endure.

Somehow I always find alternatives and loopholes to flee, but whatever decision I make, I keep finding a way to see only you, which makes me view life from an entirely new perspective, one I didn't know of before.

In the midst of my daily struggles, experiences, and methods, I get stuck when it comes to trying to make you glad. Mostly I have meant nothing and had no worth to others, not until you showed me kindness, affection, trust, and loads more.

I know I am not the perfect man or the right choice for you, as was made clear by the information you retrieved about me. Despite all the facts, I just want to let that you're the bedazzler of my soul 'til kingdom come.

At a crossroads is what I feel in your presence. A lot of ideas flow through mind, mostly good ones, but others are just downright naughty. I express them just so I can try to put a smile on your pretty face. I make a fool out of myself for the sake of humor.

Among all the gorgeous woman I see and know, I guess you have been able to rise up way above the rest, surpassing my standards.

My eyes simply picked you out of a huge crowd. Without further notice, I fell head over heels in love with you.

Praise and glory come from heaven, whereas peace and tranquility are up to people. Forgiveness is commonly given if it is sought correctly. A beauty like you is never forgotten. I say this to hint that you're the only one who has the ability to earn the key to my heart, body, and soul.

Adorable Beauty

Every day is a new chapter in everyone's life except mine. Many people do various things like work, party, joke, exercise, and a lot more, but for me it's rare to do any of those things. The only thing I like doing and will continue to like doing is just admiring an adorable beauty like you.

Honestly, however stern I may be in trying to stop myself or resist temptation in order to be close to you, it just doesn't seem to work, so I try constantly to find a solution. I come up with the answer that you're the only adorable beauty I will ever need around me.

All the events and occasions that may come to pass won't be able to dampen my feelings for you, as my heart starts beating faster when I hear your name. Recalling your beauty makes me want to explode.

If I do have to die, it won't make a difference. If you are there, then I will feel excited, loved, and like the happiest man alive.

I know the words are straightforward, but that's me. I have no hiccups or secrets when it comes to you. This is due to the mere fact that I am in love with you, my adorable beauty, and am praying hard that someday soon you'll reciprocate.

They say that every second counts. Whatever you may be doing does matter to me. The time we shared will not be back. It will end up being a fragmented memory of all the attention, care, dedication, and comfort I've shown to you and which you deserve, directly indicating how precious you are to me and that I am a nobody without you by my side.

Everlasting Dream

When people have insomnia, it is usually because they are stressed, worried, and so forth. I pledge that the only cause for my lack of sleep is that I dream of you.

Please don't ask me to explain myself, since all I know is my love for you, which will never change, hence making you my everlasting dream. I will never stop dreaming of you.

You are constantly but sweetly buzzing in mind, leading me to become distracted from the tasks at hand. But I don't care, because you are my everlasting dream, never to become a reality.

It has been proven by many that people tend to change with time, depending on stimuli or the natural aspects around them. For me, change is mainly this everlasting dream and my drive to create a solution in order to make it become the best dream I'll ever dream about. Though we haven't met, I long daily for the moment when I am able to meet you, the main reason being that I am sidetracked without you.

Everyone in the world needs someone to share their life with. Otherwise they end up being angry, agitated, lonely, and so on.

This is why I formally ask the people around me to be witnesses to a statement indicating why I choose you as my everlasting dream and why I wait for you to become a reality someday soon. We will become united by our engagement and then by our marriage vows, and then we will be able to visit the various galaxies in our immense universe.

The Purest Love
Making My
Destiny

The word *destiny* implies a lot so that people can have a clue about its significance, just like the phrase *pure love*, which up to now remains a riddle waiting for an answer. We, the starters and appliers of such words and phrases, don't know the repercussions they will have in the minds of the few who are clueless.

Though it's tough for me to elaborate on this concept, I will say that many people try to practice the interpretations of the words and phrases without seeking their meaning. In the end, these people hesitate because they are in a trance or have gone astray.

Regardless of such imperfections, all I want to tell you is that no matter how many words may be uttered by our predecessors and ancestors, you should keep remembering only the good times we shared. Discard any words that may be hurtful to you or others.

Words can be used to describe one's emotions, feelings, character, and personality (along with many other qualities), but words may simultaneously be misunderstood, which can create a conflict between the people concerned. Because of this, I implore you to acknowledge my commitment to use only passionate and respectable words when speaking to you. I will do this for all eternity.

My pride and joy can only be denoted by words shared in our conversations, letters, e-mails, poems, and so forth. I try my best to carefully filter my words when conversing with you, especially because you're the last angel I want to offend with uncalled-for words.

There are moments when I end up speechless or wordless when it comes to you, but what continues to motivate me are your gestures, ideology, perceptions, beliefs, teachings, beauty, and respect, all of which are unique and rare.

Every Time
Remembering
Only You

Days come and go. You are a unique woman. To me you're special in a way, but no one else feels you're the best because you're always around. Permit me to say that you're the best thing I could ever dream of having around me, anywhere or at any time—in this lifetime or in the ones yet to come.

Every time is a common phrase used by many to tell someone else how they feel. It is also used as an excuse when people have no words to say. For me, *every time* means when I will be there for you to help you, protect you, and care for you. I'll constantly and forever be around.

My advice is never to stop having faith. Believe, keep praying, and stick to your principles, as they will guide and protect you forever. To ensure your safety is all I have ever wanted to do for you. Well, that and much more.

Checking up on you is something that I think is great when compared to all my other daily tasks. Nothing makes me feel joy except for the seconds when I think of you and only you. The first time we met, I didn't expect that I would get close to you and continue being close to you. Every time I recall those moments, a smile spreads across my face, which is a rare occurrence. Even those who are around me at that moment in time recognize my smile and start their inquisition. My response to that is, was, and will be that you're the only one I remember every time. There is no way that I will change such happiness—not for anything—until the end of my days.

For all the suffering I may have unintentionally caused you, I sincerely seek your pardon. I am hopeful that we will rekindle that which was good and memorable. I hope that we continue to cherish the memories we share. I am, every time, remembering only you.

My Soul's Overwhelmer

There are moments and memories that are unforgettable. However much we try to resist temptation, our human nature normally decides to indulge our desires. Yet we complain that the fulfillment of our desires is not good enough to conquer and satisfy our mind, body, and soul.

The setbacks that control me when I am not thinking about you or missing you are tremendous. No doubt that it's hard to compromise the ego, but trust me, not doing so results in a pleasant scenario in the end.

All the setbacks that I have experienced because of women came about, I have realized, because they wanted chocolate, another type of candy, roses, or other nice goodies. So I then made it a point to find out the reasons for this. My conclusion is that all women are wonderful, colorful, incomparable, loving, and caring. Mostly they're all sacred to me, despite the fact that you're the best among the rest. You have overwhelmed me, regardless of the rest.

In all the times I have been around you, I've known you as a sacred person who does not compete with my heart's desire. I think you're irreplaceable. Whether I am in my right mind or not, just rest assured that you're my number one no matter what other people may say. Nothing really matters as long as you're by my side in this lifetime or the next. That's what really counts to me. Only then do I know I am complete and worthy of living. Otherwise, I end up a loser—no one but a loser with no guidance at all.

Some memories are meant to be kept; others, to be forgotten. The difference between you and the other women I know is that I will never be able to forget anything about you. You are the only memory I'll cherish until the end of my days.

Beholder of Beauty

As the night weaves its way through, you can see, if you look into the sky, lots of stuff that can't be found on earth. Never try to hide the truth. Revealing the truth is the best way to set yourself free. Being truthful also relieves you of any guilt you have. Don't think you're a detriment to the people around you. Don't judge yourself harshly. Instead, always give yourself the benefit of the doubt.

We are all different, whether good-looking or not. Just know that you're special in your own way and that nobody can change that, unless you want to yourself.

Never mind all that is happening around you. What you do and think, and how you act, is what makes you great. I am honestly pleased to meet you. Simply, without any doubt, I consider you to be all the beauty I behold.

Lonely without You

Planning my day, I found out it was no use. I knew I wouldn't keep up with the plan. Regardless, this time I decided to make the effort. Can you guess what I planned to do? Don't worry yourself too much in trying to figure out something I won't like or that will bother you in any way. To prevent you from worrying is why I am going to give you a brief description of my plan.

Basically it relates to you and is meant only for you. There is no other person I want to be with other than you, but that's not all. I arranged for us to hang out together, although it's kind of difficult. But why give up without trying? Pardon me if I was wrong to even think of such a thing. Regardless of all that, I can't bear to be without you anymore, not even for a second. I am very lonely without you.

I just gaze into the sky, during the day or the night, when I am in pain, sad, or feeling sick. Nothing else lures me. I may visit my family doctor or a specialist, but in spite of all the treatment, there is one special care I usually lack, and that is you. You're the one who relieves my heart and makes me feel at peace. Trust me, I freak out when I'm not able to think about you.

A lot is going on my mind, but never doubt me. I am sincere. You have heard plenty of negative and sarcastic remarks about me, and you still don't believe them. Furthermore, you are the only one who understands me for who I am and accepts me into your life. Thus permit me to say that I am honored to have been given the privilege to know an angel like you, who has conquered me.

There isn't anything I wouldn't do for you. I will do anything just to see your face, just to see you smile, be happy, and be relaxed—and many other good things I haven't mentioned. In my world, you're my all. I will wait for the day when you realize what you mean to me. In the meantime, all I feel and know is that I'm lonely without you.

Reviver of Love

In today's world, everyone's way of life has undergone many changes. Most people say the world is becoming a better place. There is still something that I doubt, and that is who the main instigators are that make this world a better place. I believe it's the people who reside in the world. In spite of my answer, there is something essential I need to confirm with you. All I can tell you for now is that even if the world is stagnant or people are doing what they do best to me, I'll always consider you to be a person who cannot be compared to any other.

Many people have their weaknesses and strengths. For me, I am strong and feel secure when you are near, but the second you disappear, I become weak in the sense of being lonely, upset, in pain, and sad—and other things that I can't bear to name or elaborate on.

For most of my days here on earth, I have seen things, done things, conquered things, and dealt with things, but what is missing is someone as precious as you to cuddle with, comfort, hold, protect, care for, miss, love, cherish, and hate. I pray often that I will experience such compassion with only one person in this world and that it will be you.

Nobody else has even come close to me or swept me off my feet more than you have. The only thing is that I need to have the will to wait for you and not flirt, play, or fool around with any other woman. That's not me. I am a person of principle who respects everyone's feelings, especially yours. Don't ask me to be far away from you. If you do, then I'll go insane—more than I already am—without you.

The bad things that people say or do to me are countless, but I don't give those people the satisfaction they seek. Before meeting you, though, I was different. Somehow you removed all the hatred from my soul, for which I had longed for quite a while. At least I am not holding back my true feelings for you. Remember the ring. You're the only person who made me realize the true meaning of being loved and of loving someone back. Too bad my love is meant for you. Even if you leave me, I will always love you.

Gentle Lady

One day I was demoralized, ready to give up on all that I was doing. In short, I lost faith and hope. I was lonely, hurt, and upset. No one around me could understand what I was going through. Then I prayed and felt great. I prayed to meet someone special, someone I didn't know yet who had a wish to help me get my courage back and put my life back in order. Deep down inside, I was feeling miserable solely on account of the fact that I was letting evil, instead of good, step into my life. And on that fine day, after all the hassles and struggles with those who cared about me, you appeared like a guardian angel and rescued me from disaster. All I know is that if it weren't for you, I would be a damsel in distress, having nowhere to go and no one to guide me or take care of me because I let everyone down. I wouldn't have been able to overcome all this anguish and fear without you. You are the nicest person I have ever come across. I am hoping to find a way to thank you with all my heart. I want to let you know that you're the best. God did not make a mistake by giving my life meaning through you. All I can tell you is that you're the first gentle lady I've come across. I hope you will be the last gentle lady I'll ever desire to encounter, now and until eternity.

Greatest Lifesaver

To me you're unique. You are just the one I want to have around me at all times. Even if you are not there physically, you're with me in my thoughts and prayers and whatever else I do that is especially good.

If I had had the privilege of meeting you a few years ago, my life for sure wouldn't be the disaster waiting to happen that it is now. I am currently breathless for words. I bet there isn't anyone who can really understand what you mean to me, so why should I lie to you? I know there won't be any way on earth for me to show you my utmost gratitude and appreciation, things that I will never be able to share with or give to anyone else except you. Believe me when I say this to you each time we are together. I feel like I have entered a dilemma. You are present and are holding my hand tightly so that you are able to pull me out of all the wrong I do and drag my sorrowful soul into heaven. I know for sure that I won't make it there on my own. I thank the Lord for giving me a second chance to make the effort that I need to make in conquering all of the obstacles that are in my way as I try to reach paradise. That's why he gave me the honor of meeting you, a loving, caring, sweet, pretty, adorable role model. Now I request that you help me to fulfill my dreams and make them a reality—just the way I wish them to be.

What I want to say to you before concluding my poem is that I feel the urge to live without despair. Believe me, I am prone to doing haphazard things without thinking about the consequences. And since you allowed me to become your friend, you have made me realize the greatest reasons to live, namely, to love, to give, to honor, to cherish, to conquer, to thank, to calm down, and to think. I admit that this is why I call you the greatest lifesaver of all time.

Forgive me for all of the things I have put you through all this time. Know that there isn't any other woman who will replace you in my heart. Whatever the circumstances are between us, you'll always be my number one and the greatest lifesaver of all time.

Eternal and Irreplaceable Happiness

There has always been a gap between us. We both know this. Anyway, I want to tell you that you're the best angel I've had the opportunity to know. Also, you're an inspiration. Believe me, the days I've spent with you have been the best days of my life.

You were the one to encourage me to change my ways and my expectations, which I needed to do in order to accomplish my day-to-day activities. Most of the things I do are very confusing, irritating, heartbreaking, scary, weird, and so on, but in spite of all that, my thoughts come rushing back to haunt me with the worry of how my actions affect you. You are important to me. The rest, I am not bothered about.

I don't know why I feel secure, appreciated, cared for, taken seriously, maybe missed, and glad about it without having any regrets. People say that nothing becomes a reality unless you make the effort to achieve what you desire. People also say that happiness is gained after one experiences a lot of sorrow. For me it's different, because you're always going to be the reality I need to make my dreams a reality and to progress toward my destiny, regardless of all the pain and sorrow. It will be worth the wait. I am happy when you are happy.

No words can make up for all the wrong things I have done in this lifetime, none of which have hurt me more than those that are related to you alone. I have tried countless times to at least prove to you how much you mean to me and how you have contributed to my success. Believe me, no one has ever done anything that I cherish more than what you have done for me. The only true words I can tell you are these: *I'm sincerely sorry—and thanks for being my happiness in this life.*

Without all your effort and determination, plus the precious time you spent to convert a lost soul like me (which, I assure you, is not wasted), I wouldn't be where I am now. I remember every minute with you, and every aspect of your teachings that I indirectly gained. Haven't you yet realized that I want to do something? I can. And the sky is the limit where you are concerned. You're the purifier of my soul. No one could ever teach me what you have taught me. However, many people do try to figure me out, as you yourself sometimes do. They never find an answer except the one that claims that I am crazy. I am glad to be the crazy one to those around me. I do act like it, which gives them a chance to gossip. They say that I am hateful. But I am not selfish. All their comments can go wherever they won't dent me, but the comments you make do affect me. There is no chance that I will ever hurt you on purpose, however much I do so unintentionally. I never mean to. I have a habit of freaking out, reacting in various ways, and losing my temper, but my temper has been under control ever since you entered my heart and cleansed it forever.

My Heart's Savior

I believe that yesterday you asked me how many women I love. It's true that there are plenty who seek my company, but I guess you know me better than any of them do. I choose my company based on whom I hang out with, whom I love, and whom I want to spend time with. There is only one person my heart desires, and that is you. Don't ask why. I will never be able to control my heart; it permits only you to control it.

If I had all the strength in the world to put things straight, guess what my first priority would be? I would undo all the wrongs I've done, especially to you. I know I keep hurting you over and over. Please do not deny that I am glad just to know you. You're the only one I cherish apart from God, my parents, and any others who honestly care about me.

The reason I brought you a heart-shaped ring yesterday is that I want you to protect it and care for it. I personally trust only you with my heart. To put it a better way, you are the only one my heart trusts. I am shocked by this, but when you are near, I feel peaceful, wanted, cared for, needed, and so many other things that words will never be able to express.

Now I know that I've had sweet dreams recently because God gave me an angel to be there for me every second of the day. I don't deserve it, but I am thankful for it. You are a goddess. I assure you, I will never abandon you, no matter much we fight, argue, and get angry with each other. You know that in the end I'll bow down to you and only you.

I can compare or imagine in case I collect all of the beauty life has offered me. There is no way that I'll come to doubt that you're the only one who can bring happiness to my life. We have a lot of similarities, but that's because you are everything nice that God ever made, is making, or will make, either now or for endless lifetimes to come.

Repeatedly I have weird moods. This is because of my various problems. But haven't you noticed that as soon as I see you, I am cured and back to normal? I have a bad temper; I won't refute that point. It is a weakness I am hoping to be rid of soon. Once it's gone, I'll be better off. I am kind of pledging my commitment to improve my lifestyle. You're the only one who can change me.

For you I'll do anything and give anything, because truly you're only one who brings happiness and love to my miserable life. All I can say is that you're everything pleasant and decent. On top of that, you are adorable, cute, intelligent, sexy, unique, and a princess.

There are many places, treasures, and adventures to try for, but none of them will have the effect of making me as happy as you do from a distance.

Most of the time, I like to relax, enjoy life, have fun, and party all night long. However much I try to forget the day when I saw your photograph, I still find that your methods and principles for living make me think, over and over again, what I could become if I were to follow in your footsteps.

Even if I were to be left alone for the next several days, months, or years, nothing would be able to convince me to forget the days when I dreamed of having a lifestyle like yours.

To me you're perfect. That's how I always imagine you. Before we meet, which is something I long to have the chance to do, I don't want to embarrass myself or you, so I ask in advance for your forgiveness of my imperfect words and actions.

Now I leave you with a small idea of how you have been a stepping-stone for life, for which I have waited anxiously. I thank the Lord regularly for letting me see you just once on an unforgettable day, and I thank you for helping me to make the right choice in life.

Heartfelt Emotions Meant for You

When I think of all the times we have shared, from the silly to the sad, I discover that you have been the greatest fancy face to me, through good times and through bad.

We love to get crazy from time to time. That's what loving people—you especially—are supposed to do.

But when times get rough, I never doubt that you, Fancy Face, are the one person on whom I am able to rely for anything at any time.

We have this force between us that will endure until the very end. I can't imagine my life without you.

Fancy Face

In the world of today, nothing seems to be long-lasting until it disappears. Correct me if I am wrong, but I believe that we all have the right to be free from evil. Although it's a very difficult idea that most people try their best to avoid, regardless of all the effort and sacrifices made, it is guaranteed that everyone living has done an evil deed. Whether they accept it or not, the fact remains the same.

Don't think that I am hiding anything from you. I can't hide anything from you, not even when I try. The looks you give me change my desire to be evil. Somehow I feel secure with you, which is something that I never imagined, not even in my wildest dreams. Whenever I dream of you, guess what happens? My face, my body, my soul, my heart, and all my other organs feel alive and full of happiness. Seeing you cures all my sorrows, thus making you my guardian angel here on earth. I am happier to have you more than any other treasure I seek to possess. You're my favorite person. I wish to spend every second of my miserable life with you. My apologies if I am too direct, but I will not lie to you. I don't know why anyone else would either.

So pardon me once again if I gather up all the courage I have in me and let you know in writing what you mean to me. And my condolences to you for the fact that I call you (and nobody else) Fancy Face.

By now, surely you want to strangle me, beat me up, and chase me away. At least I openly and truthfully disclose my feelings to you. I have come to the conclusion that living life without you is a waste of time and oxygen. I have committed a lot of bad deeds in the past, all of which I now regret. I am rectifying my mistakes thanks to your prayers, presence, and dedication. I will never be able to repay you. My spirit, my all, belongs to you until eternity.

I know I am not what you expect out of life, but it means a lot to me to have your beauty, joy, and peace in my life. When you are around me, all I can do is thank the Lord for giving me the honor of knowing someone as humble, dedicated, loving, and humorous as you. Fancy Face, any other guy would like to know you too.

Your Incomparable Gestures

Many times I experience a dilemma that I honestly have no clue how to solve. All know is that it is somehow connected to you. I am not disappointed or angry about this. Instead, I am happy, because it involves you and only you.

There isn't any other important person besides you in my life, however much you may try to avoid me, hate me, beat me, hurt me, abandon me, reject me, forget me, discard me, or treat me in any other way that you may think fit. Whatever you choose to do won't bother me. You're my mentor here on earth. Without you, I am useless, lonely, miserable, sad, scared, hurt, and mostly unloved and unmissed.

You think I am dishonest or playing with your feelings. Please remove those unwanted thoughts from your mind. Nothing would make my spirit more peaceful than to give you anything you may need. I would like to make you as happy as you make me.

All the words in the world won't make up for all the wrongs I have done to you, as I have done many. But I assure you now that I won't ever wrong you again. I am simply saying sorry once again. You are a blessing in disguise. I wish you knew all about my past. The Lord gave me the honor of knowing an incomparable mermaid who always makes my days worthwhile.

If I had the power to take back all my wrongs and replace them with rights, I would do it with no doubts. But for the wrongs I committed against you, I would pay the price. Every aspect of your life is my number one concern until the end of time.

Nothing can ever replace my love for you. This is a promise I make to you, on my life and with God as my witness. However much I abstain from thinking about you, there is always a stronger force that dominates me and lets you be in control, just the way I like it.

Up to now, you have been the only person whose overruling of my decisions I've accepted. I counteract anyone else who tries to tell me what to do. Believe me, you are my all. Even if someone else falls in love with me, you must know that I love you more than anything else I will ever care for, miss, cherish, think of, or pray for. Now it's your decision, not mine. I have told you the truth and am proud of it. You make me feel like I am in heaven.

The Woman of My Dreams

Since the day you crossed my path, I couldn't get your image out of my mind. Now, every second when I breathe or even try to utter a word, the only thing I speak aloud is your name, even though I never decide to say it aloud. This is mainly why I think of you as the woman of my dreams.

There are a lot of people who like to pry into other people's lives, but the only thing they pry into is the bad side of the person they decide to gossip about. All I ask of you is not to take what they say so seriously. I will always know that you are the woman of my dreams. Trust me when I say that no one could replace you, not even if they tried.

Today is the day I make a promise to love you, be with you, and honor all your desires, hopes, and needs, together with anything else I have forgotten to mention. Currently my emotions are going wild and I feel like crying. Just thinking of you makes me lose control. You're a challenge I will never be able to shake. You are the woman of my dreams. And since it is said that dreams come true, mine will come true someday soon.

The Psycho Who'll Forever Love You

There are so many things that make me want to keep you safe. To me, your safety is my security. I don't know why I feel this way, but I do know that I love every second I spend worrying about you. Nothing else makes me more active than you do.

If I were given a wish, I'd use it on you, since to me you're worth more than all the good and precious things of this world we live in. As long as I have your guidance, I have no doubt that I will avoid doing wrong. I pray daily that this will never change.

There are many people who despise me and say a lot of things about me. They ruin my reputation. I used to freak out about this until the day that you changed my lifestyle, which is something that I appreciate, but not more than I appreciate you. Nowadays I am glad to know that your dedication to me has made me a new person altogether. I wouldn't be this way if it weren't for you. All I can say is thank you. I will always be there for you.

I realize now that a few years ago my life was a mess. I was also a mess. You have always been there for me, no matter how poorly I treated you or how badly I hurt you. I am embarrassed about my past behavior and am presently doing my best to change. It's working out. My secret is your persistence.

I cannot be the one your heart desires because you keep me out of your heart most of the time. But I will never stop loving you. That's all I know. I can give you whatever you need. Someone once told me that looks can be deceiving and that money is the root of all evil. Money definitely can't buy love or happiness. Regardless of all I have and all I do, I will continue loving you until my time on earth comes to an end.

I agree that I am not great, polite, decent, or attentive, but what I do know is that nothing means more to me than you. I will give up my freedom for yours. I would even stop breathing for you. I prefer to live alone if I cannot live with you.

Frankly, there isn't anything that could make me forget you; you're the keeper of my heart.

Your latest name for me, Psycho, suits me. I like it, actually. I will honor whichever term you use to describe me. I admire your sincerity, beauty, trust, loyalty, friendliness, care, motivation, humbleness, and sacrifice. It's rare to find a person these days who has your qualities. I have regarded you as a unique princess since the first time I saw you. I will continue thinking of you as a princess until the last time I see you.

Deliberate Act of Love

Special moments in a person's life are sometimes hard to recollect because they happen rarely. They are also hard to remember because of the influence of time, which, by the way, no one can control. For sure, most of the memories, fantasies, and dreams are cherished out of compassion for one's own mortality.

To me life can be full of surprises. Mostly people tend to be positive and look for the good, but what about the best side of life? You can't expect to become good if you constantly do bad. I'm not anyone to talk, but because I sincerely care about you and want you to have a respectable and enjoyable future, I would be honored to tell you to be greedy, selfish, untrustworthy, proud, stubborn, and so on. I vow with my whole heart and soul that if you try to be these things, you will succeed without any problem or hindrance.

My life has not been the best life. But if I do say so myself, my life is better than yours. I am not judging your life, but I am taking a lot of initiative for you. Please don't ask why. All I can say is that it's a deliberate act of love toward a special person such as you. Know that I'll always be there for you whenever you call upon me: anytime, anyplace—even in the next lifetime. I also wanted to tell you solemnly that I adore everything about you. You are the best person there ever can be. In case times get hard and you want to vanish, know that it will be very difficult for you to disappear from my life. Even if you try hard, you will not succeed, because I regard all of my thoughts about you as sacred.

Days of the Month

It seems I can't get rid of the feeling of you being around me. Although things haven't been going well between us, don't think that I have lost hope for us. Even if I were told to do the impossible for you, I would do it, because, gal, you're special. I've felt this way since the day we met out of the blue. I honestly didn't expect it. From the bottom of my heart, I say that I will never do anything to displease or hurt you in any way. I'd rather die first.

You may think that I am lying to you, trying to cover up my wrongdoing. I have nothing to hide, however. I think you know that I am telling you that all of my feelings for you are true. Every day I think of you.

This is how I've spent my days without you: On the first day, I missed you. On the second, I missed you bad. On the third, I really missed you. On the fourth, I missed you a lot. On the fifth, I missed you terribly. On the sixth, I missed you very much. On the seventh, I really missed you. On the eighth, I went crazy missing you. On the ninth, I thought about you the whole day. On the tenth, I missed you more than usual. On the eleventh, I smiled when I thought about you. On the twelfth, I missed the cute things you do. On the thirteenth, I missed holding your hand. On the fourteenth, I missed your hugs. On the fifteenth, I missed you a ton. On the sixteenth, I missed talking to you about the little things. On the seventeenth, I missed your cute body. On the eighteenth, I missed you again. On the nineteenth, I missed your laugh. On the twentieth, I missed you in my sleep, in my dreams. On the twenty-first, I missed the things you do. On the twenty-second, I was counting the days until I would see you again. On the twenty-third, I missed your kisses. On the twenty-fourth, I missed you very much. On the twenty-fifth, I again missed your hugs. On the twenty-sixth, I missed you more than I had the day before. On the twenty-seventh, I missed you in the worst way. On the twenty-eighth, I missed kissing your cheeks. On the twenty-ninth, I missed giving you a big hug. On the thirtieth, I missed you more than I thought possible.

But on the thirty-first day of the month, I started praying for the day when I'd have the chance to talk, be, and laugh with you, and do the nice things that you like me to do. My love for you will exist until I die, but I was told to stay away from you. I don't appreciate such threats, but for your sake I'll do anything.

I won't be able to take it if something else happens to split us apart. You don't know what has happened to me since we last saw each other. I am glad to have known you, because you have changed me for the better. From you I learned to trust. I want to say thank you and to tell you to believe in faith and destiny. Don't let anyone or anything get the best of you.

I just wanted to be open with you. By the way, this is the best poem I have ever written. I hope you like it and cherish it just as I cherish you in my heart, even though I am abiding by what has been put forward by you-know-who. Please don't get mad. I am different, but I am not insane or foolish.

Accept me for who I am. All I know is that I love you and won't let anything bad happen to you. Even if life were to forsake us, I wouldn't abandon you in any way. As you can see, I have been keeping busy since you've been gone.

Breathless without Your Presence

All the days that I spend doing my daily activities or performing my duties, whether they are important or not, don't bother me as long as I believe that you are there to support me in all I do or plan to do in the near future. I am honestly breathless without your presence.

At any moment in your life, have you felt betrayed, been left out, been made fun of, or been seen as the dummy compared to everyone around you? If you have, that would upset me very much. If you come and try to feel what I am going through, you won't be able trust me. Until you decide to be with me now and forever, I will keep proving to myself and to everyone who doubts me that I become breathless without your presence.

They say that all good things are blessings in disguise, that whenever you are charitable to others, you're making a sacrifice to the Lord for all your wrongdoings. From my point of view it's a bit different, because all the good I might ever do is to be close to you always. Nothing will make me think otherwise. That's why I pledge my love and all of myself to you, making me indispensable to you. I am left breathless without you before me.

My Glittering Star

Every time I decided to make the effort to do something constructive, I automatically went ahead with whatever was on my mind. I didn't bother myself with who was around, and I didn't care whom I was offending. I didn't give my mind even a second to adjust to the various living expenses I was amassing. Also, I did not seek help from anyone.

Many years have passed. I have performed the same old routine. I have plenty of memories, but I won't be able to hold on to them for much longer, mainly because I have a lot of unintended thoughts that dominate my reasoning ability and cause me to misperceive reality.

I felt like I dropped out of reality. I was depressed, was emotionally frustrated, and hated myself. Believe me when I say that ever since I crossed your path, a mere glance at you has helped me to forget all my worries. The brightness in your eyes has blessed me and made me renounce evil acts. Your voice has calmed my soul. From that point on, nothing has been the same with me. I changed my lifestyle. Because of this, I named you my glittering star on earth, which keeps me warm and safe all the time.

All my moments between daybreak and bedtime became full of joy, peace, and motivation. I once thought that this was too bizarre to be true. All I could think in response to that was, *Don't thank me. Thank my glittering star, who brightens my path better than the rest.*

These good and wonderful memories I have of you entering my life are still with me. I assure you that with me is where they will stay until the day I leave this earth. All I know is that without you I wouldn't be able to succeed. You're my glittering star that shines brighter during the day than it does at night. Maybe when I am asleep it watches over me.

As of now, I surrender my deepest feelings for you. I have had them for a very long time but never had the courage to confide in you. You poured your magic powder on me, cleansed my soul, cured my pain, and gave me everything a person needs. All I can do is to admit that you're the one giving person who fills me and makes me complete.

The Only One My Soul Needs

As time passed by, plenty of essential thoughts came to my attention, so I stopped and decided to take charge of my life calmly and to motivate myself to be positive, which I had done once, before disaster struck, taking me by surprise. Believe me, I had been near the point of giving up on life. Most of all, I had criticized myself for existing.

You may not understand what I was going through at that moment in my life. It was the scariest moment I have ever experienced. It felt like I was in a slumber and there was no way I could recover, until that second, which I will cherish for the rest of my life, when your image appeared in my mind and I got energy as if from nowhere. Up to now it has been a quest I haven't figured out. I hope that someday I will figure it out, with you by my side.

The first time I met you, I got a feeling I had never felt before, although it was a sweet feeling and, at the same time, just a figment of my wild imagination. I thought to myself, after a lot of hardships and suggestions for improvement that others gave to me about you, that I had not ever encouraged those people or considered even for a moment a single thing they told me about you. Don't ask me how or why; all I know is that my mind was stunned. My heartbeat was going so fast that I nearly collapsed. Shockingly, my soul decided that it needs only you in life. I believe that most everything in a person's life can be replaced by technology and the products of other scientific research. I don't involve myself in such things, because I put my stock in faith and destiny. Since my soul has never misled me, I want to admit right now that you're the one, the only one, my soul needs. I knew this from the time I first met you. I need you now and for the rest of the time I have left in this world.

To me, you are my everything. Nothing will ever be able to change the true and sincere feelings I have for you. Nobody else has ever conquered me with her trust, sincerity, beauty, confidence, affection, care, and love, none of which I ever got from, or shared with, anyone but you.

Daydreams about You

Daydreaming is a good activity to engage in once in a while. It's a rare phenomenon too vast to understand. Daydreaming tends to confuse me, because it stimulates a lot of premonitions that are really difficult to explain. All I know about the matter is that once I start daydreaming, I become lost and don't hear or feel anything around me. I like daydreaming because it allows me to become lost for a long time. It tends to awake fantasies, which I long for to become real.

The act of daydreaming is a sign of idleness, boredom, stress, loneliness, fear, and other negative things, I've learned from observation. I can vow that daydreaming has brought me to a stage in life where I am more aware of all the stuff that's happening around me. Fortunately, daydreaming affects me differently compared to most people. I interact with my daydreams. They give me a chance to explore life in a way that is psychological and imaginative.

For a long period of time, I have tried to track down the basic reason why I like to daydream. After a thorough investigation, I came to the following conclusion: the reason I daydream is because of you. It happens more when I am alone, sad, upset, or furious, but as soon as I begin thinking or dreaming about you, all my fears flee. I don't know what I can do to stop daydreaming. I haven't succeeded thus far. In the meantime, I am trying my best to control myself, but I end up failing in anything else I am supposed to do.

When I am able to reorganize my life to improve my situation and to make myself become calmer and more optimistic, my thoughts properly focus you. I know I will never be able to repay you. Pardon me if I fail to stay away from you. It's up to you whether you want me around or not. I rest assured that I have been able to confess my ups and downs to you, the most precious angel I long to stand by and with for the rest of my life.

The Cutest Smile of My Life

Before going to bed at night, I try my best to close my eyes and forget about all the days that were meaningless to me. Nothing seems to be going right with me these days. However much I make an effort, it's like there is a force around me that is doing what it can to make my life a mistake and a living hell.

After I struggle a long time, tossing and turning in my bed, an image out of nowhere appears. It looks so real that I sit up and try my best to catch it in my hand. It seems to be very close, but it is very far away. At last I figured out why I was getting confused, delusional, and filled with rage: because something essential to me was leading me away from my Lord and my family. The only person who wasn't on my mind was you.

I won't be able to defend myself, but I do ask for the chance to explain that I wasn't being weird or insane after I trusted in you and told you that I was not thinking of you. It won't really matter, because you're the one person in this world whom I cherish, not only with my heart but also even with my breath. This is the reason that we, our souls and spirits, should be together. Without you by my side every second, I am lost to the world. That's why I don't think of you all the time, because it hurts me not to see you, hold you, protect you, care for you, and do whatever you need me to do. I hope that now you will understand why I do such things like not think of you. You're the one person whom I will never be able to forget, abandon, or lie to. You are not physically here, but I know, based on love and hope, that you're the person who has the most space in my body, heart, soul, and spirit.

If I could be granted a favor from the Lord, you know what I would ask—something that would make me happy? I would ask to see you happy, peaceful, adorable, and talented. There is nothing that I want more in this world than you.

Obstacles might be put between us. These serve as a trial, to test how much I have really learned and how much I want only you to accompany me. I would give up anything just to have a second chance to be close to you.

Evil-Deed Destroyer

Be it early morning, noon, or night, I don't tremble. The only reason that comes to mind for why I feel this way is that deep down within my soul, there is an immense amount of happiness. I have never before felt this happy with anyone else. I know life is a mystery full of challenges and commitments. No matter how much I try to stay away from you, I just can't bear the torture of it. It hurts me a lot.

Before I begin my day, I thank the Lord for giving me, a lame person who doesn't even deserve to know you, you. But never mind all the shit you may hear about me. I have realized that in life there are plenty of obstacles. Most of people's gossip about me is based on jealousy, mistrust, and disloyalty. My enemies like to interfere with my welfare.

At the beginning, it used to affect me a lot. I would give in to the comments, sarcasm, and lies, which caused me to get into trouble with the people involved.

Once I came to know you, I was glad of it, because I began trusting you, confiding in you, and trying my level best to reassure you in any way possible. For a fact, I've never done those things with anyone else. Nobody but you has made me change for the better. There isn't anything I can say or do to repay you for performing a makeover on my life. It really was the best thing I could do with my life, and it's all thanks to you, my only evil-deed destroyer.

Pardon me if I have in any way offended you or hurt your feelings. Just telling the truth about how you have changed my life for the better—which, by the way, is something that I will always treasure—makes me feel good. I plan to continue on with my new lifestyle just because it came from you. You're a person who, Lord willing, will forever be in my heart, soul, and spirit.

Heart's Consoler

I don't know what people get out of agreeing that the night is young. I just don't get it. Up to now I was kind of hoping that you would be the one to help me in my quest. I don't like leaving things unsolved.

As I continue wracking my mind for an answer, a totally different one comes to mind, and that is that you are my heart's consoler, an insight that seriously stuns me.

Right now my mind and heart are in conflict. My emotions are running wild. My blood pressure is way beyond the limit. I've never been in this situation before. All I know is that I can't stop thinking of you. I feel at peace whenever I am thinking about or imagining you.

Believe me, that's all I can say to defend myself against any accusation brought against me concerning you as my heart's consoler. You have mesmerized me completely. It would take great effort for me to stay away from you one second longer.

Forgive me if I have crossed the line. The thing is that I am just telling you what my heart wants, no more and no less, the whole truth and nothing but the truth. I don't want to have a scare. I don't want to stay away from you anymore.

Up to now, I have never been able to confide in anyone. I have confessed everything to you, even the fact that I need to concentrate if I am going to do anything. I need you more than I need myself. No offense, I hope, exists between us. I hope that what we go through is better than what other couples go through in their relationships. I hope that we have trust and cooperation. It isn't a crime to be available to fall in love. I request your heart.

Grief Relaxer

There isn't a soul that doesn't have grief and misery. Grief is like a disease that doesn't have a cure. For me, it's you who makes me fight. I have grief. I don't know what to say anymore. I am short on words to explain why I feel the way I do about you. I know you are my grief relaxer. You have been so since the very first day I met you.

All of my friends think that being around me when I go crazy is better than being around me when I am content with my life.

I am around. I take some medication that is essential for me to function. The medicine boosts my motivation to make me think of you more often when I am alone. I am very grateful for the pills.

In public, I become very gracious, trying to stay out of people's way. What I do is stay in a spot that few people stand in—they just pass by. I wait just in case my ideal person appears. You did come by and, well, now we can spend our life together, sharing our grief and the things that we go through daily.

I play every day. When I play alone, which, to be honest, is most of time when I'm at home and you aren't around, I can't bear the fact that you aren't there. I feel that I must come and get you, as if you are away in a different country.

There isn't anything I have to offer you other than myself. I am a simple guy who appreciates kindness. It is my reason for going on in life. It stimulates my adrenalin to compare my targets. I attribute all the changes in my life to you, my grief relaxer, who rolls in to take over whenever I ask my mind, body, and soul to look upon you.

Gracious Time Spending

Today when we met in a way that we never meet, I found it to be more intriguing than usual. I honestly never expected for us to bump into each other at the diner. Don't think anything bad. It was just supposed to be me.

Frankly, I am very honest for no particular reason. You must be thinking, *Has this guy lost his mind?* Believe me when I say that I think I have lost my mind. I am trying to relax myself.

I am very confused. I must explain. All I know is that your image contributes to the difficulty in my mind, haunting me more than I am already haunted.

Never before have I ever felt so much preciousness. I am proud to know that it's you who is giving this start to my emotions—and at a price I can afford.

Whenever there is anything wrong, I get this hard image in my mind, which leads me to wake up from dreamland

and go after you. I keep going until I catch up with you, because, God, you're my heart's rhythm. I will do it for you.

Most of the time, I am a guy who likes keeping the setbacks I experience to myself. I don't like burdening anyone when I feel as if I am in a dream from which I never want to awake. I care for only you. The full of extent of my dream is to go beyond the maximum. Thank for you participating. I am the best man alive.

I honor you with my soul. Some say that you the only one who has been able to transform me and make me become special.

Uplifter

As I stand here in my room looking around, I see a lot of unwanted stuff that I ought to have disposed of a long time ago. There is always the thought of, *Live now. You can attend to those things later.* But believe me, once later comes, it doesn't come back again. In short, what I am trying to say is that somehow you have crossed my path and I want the selfsame thing as you do, which I couldn't admit before because of my pride and stubbornness. But permit me to tell you now that you're my uplifter, the only one I will never need.

Don't think that I came here trying to get your affection or anything like that. I bet you can offer it to me without any doubt—absolutely. I am not the kind of guy who keeps hope alive for people like you. You are a rare breed of person, a type that can't be found just anywhere. I gladly admit that you are my uplifter. I would like to have you around all the time.

There is nothing that can make this sadness and depression go away. There is a way for me to control my temper, which makes me feel insane regardless of all of my downfalls. All I have to do to recover is to remember that you are with me. When I do this, I am cured. That's the main reason why I consider you to be my uplifter. You change my life for the better.

You have the quality of purity. Trust me, friend, I would like to have nice things surrounding me so that I could have the chance to cleanse myself and become pure. And maybe, hopefully, you'll continue to be my uplifter, raising me up from a fearful boy to a courageous man.

If I had the ability to pour my heart out to you, I would do it so that you would remove all the unwanted funk and make me a new person, one whom anyone would want to be around.

Moment of Joy

As I stare at the sky, I see a lot of greatness, as if all my problems have been vacuumed up from my mind and soul. Don't ask me why I decided to say those thoughtful words that meant a lot to you. I know that you are gone and are never coming back.

I just hate where my current thoughts—figments of my imagination, flashbacks, and other emotional ruminations—are leading me to. My only solution, and the only motivation I had, was you. Life for me now is just full of ups and downs. If I try to wash away all the great times we've had since we met, especially the days when you wore black (that was and still is your favorite color; I understand that your preference is for wearing blue these days), and you want to know why, then I'll tell you that it's really simple. I'll try my best to explain it in writing. This is the most decent thing I could come up with. Trust me, it's from my heart.

They say that when you love someone special, you feel lost, ruined, helpless, and lonely. But, woman, there has always been something that pulled me toward you: the way you dressed in black, which suited you and made me fall head over heels in love with you and gave me delightful thoughts of praise and moments of happiness. It's all thanks to you. As time went on, we went our separate ways. I don't know why. I still miss the times we shared together. Nowadays I wish I had the power to turn back the hands of time and bring you back. It's tough for me. These days I like to be wearing blue, because when I look up into the sky, I know you are looking down at me. I will wait anxiously to meet you again someday. You're the one glorious being who swept away all of my suffering and sorrow. You never knew this because I kept it all to myself. Now that you are gone physically, you are forever in my mind, body, and soul, where will be together until our next lifetime. You are and will always be the best thing that ever happened to me.

Out of Control

In the beginning, I was more or less a head-in-the-clouds type of guy. I did weird things and was totally messed up. Actually, I would call myself a crackpot or worse. I didn't like who I was.

When I was trying to develop my ability to go deep within my inner self, my hands began to unravel my weakness, which was silently destroying me.

You didn't know me at the time when I was still finding out the good and bad about myself. For no good reason, I didn't like affection. I decided it was time to change for the better. I discovered something, essentially that I was out of control and stubborn. I lacked self-control. Let's not forget that I was in denial.

If you had taken more of an interest in my life, then you would have found out that I was missing a reason to live and that I wanted to love and, in return, be loved. In spite of all my shortcomings and downfalls, I never gave up hope. Something kept the spirit within me alive. It was you, my sweetheart. In your own special way, you took away my insecurities and paid me attention, which I hadn't ever wanted before.

Now I don't know where else I could have gone or, even better, what I could have done with myself if it weren't for you coming into my life and rectifying it once and for all. There isn't any way I can repay you, either with gratitude or in kind. All I know is that I am forever indebted to you.

You are divine, the blessing in disguise I had been longing for all of my life. Apart from my parents, who gave me their all as well, you are the only one who took all of my psychotic, out-of-control behavior and replaced it with love, gentleness, appreciation, and other good things that are too numerous to jot down. I just want to clear the air between us. I want to make things work out for the both of us so we can start afresh.

My soul is confident that this can be accomplished.

Narrow-Minded

Time is something that no one, none of us here an earth, can control. Time, like our hounding thoughts, is a figment of the imagination. The difference is that time is uncontrollable, but thoughts are always adjustable according to a person's capability and motivation. Honestly, you are the first person I have looked at without appearing punishing in an old-fashioned way or seeming narrow-minded about the situation. In trying to figure out what it was, in the end all I came up with is that you, no one else, make me feel alive. I am physically active once again since the Lord is with me spiritually. With that said, you could be here with me mentally.

For me, for us, there is a challenge. I won't give up, because deep down inside I have a sense of reality I have never been able to express before. It's more than a fact that makes me act better and more honorably. It also brings about happiness, joy, freedom, affection, and care. I wouldn't be able to explain, not even if I tried.

Every person has a right to express his or her feelings and opinions, although I don't think that anyone should offend their neighbor by doing so. I was assessing my situation and came up with the belief that my savior is here on earth. Right then, I realized that my life is better. There is no person I have met, or will meet in the near future, who can compare to you. I have the courage to thank you well in advance for helping me to stop thinking and doing things narrow-mindedly and to help me start thinking and doing things cooperatively and with commitment instead.

Mesmerized by Your Fragrance

To me, a blessing is very important, regardless of where or whom it comes from. All that really matters is how you accept, appreciate, and cherish what comes, regardless of any emptiness or remorse you may feel for not overcoming a weakness. The best thing to do is to forgive and forget, and then bless that person and all that you have. For me to succeed in life and in my position, which I was forced to contend with after meeting you, I decided to pray for you to continue being in my life. It is a blessing for me to be with you. The feeling that I get from you is intensified by the fragrance of your perfume. Actually, that's just a cover-up for the loneliness I feel for you.

Every morning before starting my day, I thank the Lord for having given me the privilege of meeting such a dazzling beauty as you. Believe me, I hadn't expected it to happen. Since the day I met you, I've had to corner my thoughts about and feelings for you. I can't shake them out of my mind. This makes me mesmerized not by your fragrance but by your kindhearted act, which made me fall madly in love with you.

Most people usually plan their days after looking at a calendar. I plan my day daily. The only thing I like planning is how I am going to win just a second more of your company so that I can assure myself, although you are far away, of how much I love you. I will be able to consider myself whenever, not just this morning, based on the mere fact that you're the one who has been able to mesmerize me by your fragrance. I tell you solemnly that this will never change.

Cradle of Trust

A long time ago I was having a flashback of all my deeds, both good or bad, and came to the conclusion that I was alone and without companions, so I forced the question on myself, asking, "Why are you alone?" And a voice, I guess it was imaginary, told me tenderly, "You not alone. I care for you." Straightaway, I sensed something in my spirit and mused that the voice was definitely yours.

Many events have happened. In a way, you, like the only light in a dark home, are the only one who is able to understand me. I have been able to consider this, and I know that there is nobody else who can do it. I can tell you anything that has happened to me without feeling any doubt at all. You have always been there for me. Please permit me to say that you are my cradle of trust. I am very glad to know that you are the loving person for whom my soul longs.

Relationships are very interesting. When a relationship you are in is right, your heart regards it as a gift. A relationship can be very enjoyable if it is taken seriously, or very demoralizing if it is misused. According to my point of view, I'd like to have a long relationship with you, with no cross words or squabbling to make up for. I wanted to discover what you meant to me after I considered all aspects of our relationship, everything that we have been through in our lives. I came up with this: you are my cradle of trust. No other woman can replace you. May you be number one in my life until the end of time.

Dream Companion

I was busy doing my work on a laptop. It fluently came to my mind that I was relaxed. You have never had a thought such as this one. This idea dazzled me for quite a while. I recalled the particular moment when guilt came over me. I was feeling dread, but I also felt glad. I wanted the moment never to end. I am glad that I continued on with my dream.

For an hour after that, I forgot all about the demands of my work. I was at this time lying down in my bed and reading. I fell asleep. When I awoke, I hoped you were really there. I guess that was too much to expect. Anyway, I loved it.

Please don't ask me the reason why I choose you mainly in my dreams. Maybe you could someday help me to figure this out—and also help me make my fantastic dream come true.

Generally I get a grace period when I love. I also get the honor of dreaming. Most of the time, I am working, studying, or helping to do well in my supervisory position, but all of this is minus one very important thing, which is spending time with you, the one who wakes me from my dream. Now, since I've finally given you my time and told you my side of the story of what's really happening in my life, I am planning to make you my number one priority. Now you can be my dream companion fully until the end of time.

Wherever I dream of you, something changes from wrong to right. I feel alive, happy, peaceful, and reformed—things that a man feels when he wants a dream to become a reality.

You are the best dream any guy could ever ask for. I hope that you will feel the same way soon. I confess that I believe that no one can correct the dream, no one but us.

Evictor of Sorrow

Every moment in time, something is always going on with us. It is better for everyone if all is going well, but in my case I have a life that is deteriorating on account of many circumstances, setbacks, criticisms, and all the other shit that can make a person go mad.

All I am trying to say is that all lives are different and none of them result in perfect happiness, freedom, and enjoyment. There is often something missing in my life. I realize that it's you and nobody else.

I agree that for most of my days here on earth, I have done more bad than good. I have assessed this. Regardless of the fact that I am focused on the humdrum, I still have what I need to move on with the fight, partly because I see a great, powerful gateway to the future. I am assuming that my future will be with you, my evictor of sorrow. With you, I may look forward to a bright and everlasting future.

People around me tell me about how they've experienced various challenges in their daily struggles with life. This has kind of given me a way to choose good or bad. Trust me when I say that you are the one who stimulates my interest and gives me the hope I long for each and every second, so that I am able to overcome anything in my way without any difficulty. I am trying to tell you that you're the only evictor of sorrow I will ever need.

For memory's sake, I will tell you this in the best possible way without making you feel bad. I am honored to have a blessing like you in my life. I am very proud of you. You're my only and eternal evictor of sorrow. No one else could ever replace you, even if I had a choice.

Crazy about You

One fine day I was trying to gather up all the events and occasions I've experienced, all the memories I've had, all the acts and deeds I've done, and all the advice that others have given to me. I was stunned to discover that I'd missed the best, which is your tender love, affection, and smile, along with your beauty, commitment, opinions, and laughter. Even though everything else was said to me by others, I accepted and thanked them all. Then I paused for a second and began praying. Don't ask why, as I can't explain. It just came into my subconscious mind. You are the reason I was praying. I was asking for forgiveness for having forgotten to consider your feelings. This upset me more than anything else ever could have. I messed everything up because I am crazy.

If I were given all the nice things of this world, everything that a man could ever dream of having, there is nothing that would be more worthwhile to me than to have you by my side at all times. I feel an extraordinary sensation within me wherever I am doing something and simultaneously missing you. I wish I had the ability to ignore what was going on. It will be unbelievable to you, I presume, but it's a simple fact that you're the most important thing to me. I regard you as being more important than I am. I wish I could change what I feel for you, but it's impossible. I will remain crazy about you regardless of any hindrance I may face.

Pardon me if I have offended you in any way. To me, speaking the truth is the easiest and safest way to avoid confrontation, disbelief, insults, and so on. I really wouldn't mind if you didn't forgive me. From my restless soul, body, and mind, I make the plea that we resolve our previous anger, which we may still have, and concentrate on what is ahead. For the record, you are way beyond anybody else. You always will be. This might make you understand why I love you and am crazy about you.

Delusional

Earlier today, just before I left the office, a sudden shower came. I was feeling cold, empty, weak, sad, and emotional. Please don't ask me how or why. I remain stunned by the whole scene. I am not myself, I guess, since I am so confused right now and don't know how to embrace you. Thus I am informing you, hinting to you, that I am delusional without you.

Recently I have noticed that no matter what time of day it is, I have a passion for being around you. I want to be with you every second of the day. You could say that I am losing my mind, but trust me when I say that it would be worth it to me if I did lose my mind in exchange for your happiness. All I am implying is that you're the most important thing in my life. Nothing and no one can replace you or keep me away from you. In any case, I just wanted to tell you that I have a delusional longing for you to be close me.

People are all around us in life. I treasure these people with all my heart. Without you, I feel pain in my chest, like a knife has ripped through my heart. Anything is just a milestone, which people offer as an excuse after performing a task. The major difference between me and others is that I like taking risks, because I am delusional and proud to have you on my mind at all times.

Days, time, years, and many other things are present in my life, but I believe without any doubt that you're the only source of joy to my soul. But you're missing, and honestly I become very delusional wherever you're not around.

Before you try to judge or criticize me, please take a minute to consider my hope, joy, and feelings. Gal, without you making me delusional, my daily activities are definitely incomplete.

Gentle Day

One day I was demoralized and gave up on everything I was doing. In short, I lost faith, hope, and everything worth believing in. In time this made me become lonely, hurt, and upset. Trust me when I tell you that I was like on outsider in my own home. No one could understand what I was going through at that particular time in my life. I couldn't explain how I felt at that time. If I were asked to elaborate, I wouldn't even know how to begin.

I am very thankful to the Lord for giving me the courage, ideas, and strength I needed to get along more peacefully with others and with myself. Time elapsed. My prayers were consuming me more than I had imagined they would. What I prayed for daily was to find a special person like you to be my companion through all my struggles and in my suffering, happiness, and laughter.

These thoughts are actually meant to bring peace to you. To me you're like a guardian angel who took the time, and had the patience and understanding, to comfort me, a poor, deranged person in distress. There is no way I know of to repay you for making sacrifices on my behalf. I know that I can really be a pain. None of my words or actions will change what you mean to me. Only faith and destiny will be able to guide me daily.

I know that you came into my life not by mistake but as a blessing. You are a motivator, trying to bring quality to our life. You personally changed my life for the better. I won't be able to physically show you my appreciation for your generous gestures, but I can let you know that you're the only great woman I wish to have in my life. You're my number one, nobody else.

People tend to brag about the various things they have. Sometimes they do have these things. Mostly these people merely want these things. They are poseurs. They know they aren't able to have what they want. But when it comes to lonely people like you, it is a must that you be treated with decency, respect, care, and humility, as a lovely person like you deserves these things. You're my sacred treasure. I will never give you up. I wouldn't trade you for anything.

If something or someone is bothering you in any way, please don't hesitate to inform me. My main purpose is to ensure that you're all right at all times. This is what really matters to me—more than any other thing, including my daily activities.

There isn't any way for me to describe your beauty, style, intelligence, and articulateness. Believe it or not, I have found no flaws in you. I am trying to admit to myself that you are perfect in all ways. I personally feel it is necessary to say that you're the only sacred treasure I will ever need if I am to conquer this confusing situation that I find myself in.

For all the time that I have been alone, just wasting to start afresh and bury the past, there has been one memory that has grabbed my attention. I just can't forget it, not even if I were brainwashed. You are the only sacred memory I have. I honestly am not able to forget you even though you've gone and moved on. I wish we could meet again under better circumstances.

Desired Destiny

Actually I don't know why I got the thought of writing about destiny, because I know and believe that none of us on earth can predict where our destiny will take us. But I was planning all day, and all I came up with was the word *destiny*.

Trust me when I tell you that I didn't believe in destiny until the day you crossed my path. Maybe it was a coincidence, or maybe it was a sign from heaven telling me not to give up hope and faith but to gain the courage needed to cope with all that I may face.

Since that day happened and my thoughts and acts changed easily, I started believing (wrongly) that something had entered me and was now constantly inside me. I felt like I was possessed by a spirit that lifted me up to defend all good deeds and to stop all bad deeds.

I don't know how you relate to what I just wrote above, but I am glad to know that it is you who makes me to better organize my thoughts. You definitely give life to me. How much this world needs me! How best can I act in order to make life feel better, not only for me but also for all the rest, including you?

By the way, if I were to ask you how you would feel if someone asked you about yourself and your desires, what would you reply? When you have the answer, please don't think twice. Just find a way to let me know. To me, you're very classy and endearing. I would give anything to have you by my side. That's why I have gained the courage and started to love faith. With this, I am letting you know that you're the only destiny I desire. Now and forever I will need to live a focused life, as my best days are yet to come.

Gal, on the first day we met, we became friends. My heart started pumping harder than ever before. Maybe I was imagining it. But it really didn't bother me since it was a response to your presence.

All I want to ask of you is that you help me gain clarity about such a significant experience in my life, something I'd never experienced before, of having such a wonderful beauty in front of me and finding that my heart began beating hard—just like when a person becomes excited by a pleasant gesture or emotion.

Regardless of all that I have said above, I have been nursing a thought, constantly thinking about it. Believe me when I tell you that I wasn't really aware until the day I saw you beside me chatting, giggling, having fun, and most of all sharing your thoughts, telling me about your hobbies, and discussing your ups and downs. Best of all, we expressed all our feelings openly without any barriers between us, like friends who love each other more than faintly.

If we should encounter obstacles on the way to our destiny, don't worry. I believe that obstacles are only a test of faith. God wants us to decide whether we can put our love for each other to the test of faith. This will prove whether we are compatible with one another or not.

Every day the sun rises in the east and sets in the west. I am not bothered in the least about where the sun rises or sets. What concerns me is what's going on in your life and how I can best be used to ease any burden or worry you may face. I am always going to be there for you. I will treat all your tasks as my first priority.

Imaginary Guardian Angel

Thank you for being around me. Although we have not met in person, I really appreciate your being there at all times. Just by your being around amid my daily dos and don'ts, I have come to concentrate and focus more on my career.

There aren't any words I can use to describe what you are to me and how much I look up to you as a role model for my life, which honestly would be a mess if it weren't for my thinking about you or imagining that you are an angel sent with the duty of guarding me and turning me into a person of dignity, charity, respectability, and other things that are nice.

In case things get different or we have any bad luck, know that I will never come to think of you as being only imaginary. Without you, I would be lost, demoralized, and crazy. Thanks to you, my life is worthwhile.

Life is a challenge for everyone. I am be proud to have received such a precious gift from the Messiah, whom no one has seen. It is predicted that he will come again.

As stated above, what I long for is to be given the privilege to acquire you. I want you more than I want any material objects or treasures, which I wouldn't pay much attention to. I pay attention only to you and God Almighty.

I consider you to be an aide of the Messiah. You are set a little bit apart from him, but he is followed by you and only you. No one else might understand this, but to me you're the only being who has taken the time, and shown the patience and care, to support me at all times. Hence, I am forever indebted to you.

Perfect Resemblance

Every day at the break of dawn, most people tend to expect that they will do well in their work, but what people don't realize is that how they attain things in life is by being thankful for their position, which leads others to respect them and think well of their character. This leads people to refrain from making a bad impression on the general public.

As a vote of confidence, which I definitely give to you, I believe that you wouldn't undermine me if you heard any negative comments about me, such as something about my imprisonment or anything else that could tarnish my reputation. Even if you do, I know you will find a way to change my wrongdoings and guide me on the right path, since you bear a perfect resemblance to my guardian angel, with whom I long to rest.

They say it takes a while, many years, to get to know someone properly. I, on the other hand, wouldn't bother finding out about you sooner, simply because I have good faith in you. No one can ever erase or delete the feelings I have for you.

We as people face challenges that serve as guidelines to help us to understand that we should never cheat, lie, or do other bad shit. If anything, doing those things makes other people look down on you, which makes it harder for you to find joy, love, and happiness.

The secret of success isn't just hard work. It also includes motivation, interest, confidence, and belief, which, by the way, can only be attained when people are considerate of one another, share mutual affection, and cooperate with another. Now I want to tell you that all the success I have now and might have in the near future is because of your perfect resemblance to a guardian angel, which belongs to you and nobody else.

You are the only being who gives me strength, courage, and a spiritual boost. This makes people be grateful to me. I can't thank you enough, but I will try my best to repay you for all of your perfect deeds, even though what I do for you will never compare to what you have given to me and what you have made me become. I trust you completely and accept that what is happening is for the best.

Best Moment

I can't imagine a person who has no good times to remember or cherish. What really counts is how people deal with and appreciate good times.

Not all people have been blessed by a spoonful of good luck and an acceptable life. My life, for instance, is a total disaster. In spite of what I go through daily, I have tried to reorganize my life in such a way so as to satisfy the people around me, not myself. I prefer giving, helping out, and looking for justice. I am trying to say that what I really enjoy is the time I spend with you. I consider those times to be the best moments of my life.

I don't know what has happened to me since I came to find a friend whom I honor, treasure, and care for. I will do anything that is possible for me to do. I would try to make you happy at all times if only I knew what you desired.

Just as I regard my religion as holy, I treat you as holy, because that's how important you are to me. I'm not able to find the difference between holy moments and the moments I share with you, because the latter, gal, are the best moments I have ever experienced. I hope to ensure that they will never disappear, like most things in my life do.

Surprises come from nowhere. We have no clue when they will come along in life. There is plenty of joy, laughter, and so on. This is how I picture you: as a surprise, but better, hence adding to my fear of losing the best moments of my life. You're the leading lady in my life. Nothing will ever change that.

Affixed Memory

Whenever I am around people, I begin to shiver. I feel a cold breeze following along my spine. When I concentrate a little bit more, why, it happens that your beautiful face appears in my mind. I am trying to move on, but trust me—it's just too difficult.

If there were a tactic available to make me forget your memory, I wouldn't make use of it. Nobody but I can justify this. All I am trying to say is that you are one affixed memory I wouldn't want to part with, not even for a second.

When you were around, I felt complete and became a grateful man. Many of the friends I used to hang out with before meeting you were stunned about my new attitude and behavior, which you made possible, thereby saving me from having an idle mind and having no objective in life.

Now you are gone, and for sure I know you won't be coming back in this lifetime, but I constantly wish to meet you again soon. When you left, I lost something important that I will never be able to get back, at least not in this lifetime. That's for sure.

Because you were once present in my life, a fact I always regard with care, there isn't a moment when I have a second thought about you or doubt you in any way. When I lived with you, I felt like I was living in heaven. You conquered my soul, which, by the way, isn't an easy thing to do.

Recently I remember the past, especially the times we shared together. If it was only for a few hours, it was more than enough. You're an affixed memory that will never fade. I hope that wherever you are, you will help me find happiness just the way you do when we were together. I wish I was with you now. Until we cross paths again, know that I believe we can fulfill our dreams.

Printed in the United States
By Bookmasters